you are in my heart...

Us!

Celebrating the Power of Friendship

Mary anne radmacher

Us!

Celebrating the Power of Friendship

Mary Anne Radmacher

Conari Press

First published in 2011 by Conari Press,
an imprint of Red Wheel/Weiser, llc
With offices at:
665 Third Street, Suite 400
San Francisco, CA 94107
www.redwheelweiser.com

ISBN: 978-1-57324-480-0

Library of Congress Cataloging-in-Publication Data
available upon request

Cover and text design by Liz Kalloch
Typeset in Charlotte and American Typewriter.

Printed in Hong Kong
GW
10 9 8 7 6 5 4 3 2 1

especially for

_____

from

_____

Friends. Just evoking the word calls to mind the many dear souls who have been called, "friend" in my life. In some instances it was just me and a friend. Sometimes there were a handful of us, and still other times there was a whole tribe of us. In all instances I recall the "us" of my friendships, and that is one of the sweetest elements. In that sense of "us" there is a certain strength. Such diverse people and yet each friendship has brought to my life a certain strength and unique lessons and gifts.

I cannot count the number of times I have moved. So many objects have come and gone though my possession. I can, however, walk you through numerous artifacts that each hold a profound history because they have each come to me through the hand of a friend. I have a book on friendship from Maureen in 1973. While Maureen no longer stands in my life that book remains on my shelf. A steadfast reminder of our time standing as friends – that book is a warm coat I can wear on cold days.

May this book represent the treasured wealth you hold in the "us" of your friendships. May you use the abundance of thought and heart in these words as a way to reflect on your part in your friendships and gift and honor those who are a part of who you mean when you talk about "us." When we have a circle of friends, we have more fun. We get more done, we feel and are stronger and we really do celebrate the power of our "us."

You hop?

I'll skip.

You jump?

I'll fly.

I fall?

You'll catch me.

Is there a place for dreaming
where teddy bears are kings?
Where friends are the best rulers
of time and simple things?

Is there a place for hiding
from the worries of the day?
To never have to question
if I'm walking the right way?

Is there a place of wonder
where dreams are held so high?
That could I reach further my
heart would touch the sky?

There is a place where dreams are born
and thrive in safety, fair.
Where awe's alive in every breath...
our friendship takes us there.

Well, there you are...

...One day when I wasn't looking
you became my friend.

And there you go
flying another rainbow show.
It's been one of the best surprises
of my life... there you were!

When I least suspected
I turned around
and found a friend.

Stand often in the
company of dreamers...

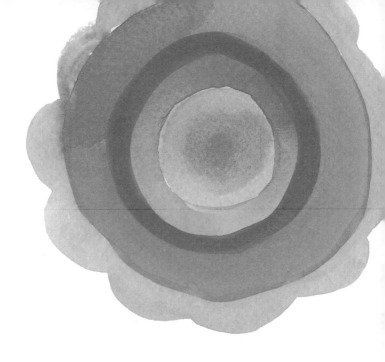

They tickle your common
sense and believe you can
achieve things which appear
impossible.

Heroic acts

and simple gestures

offer the same answer,

" Because you are my friend. "

The story
of life
is told
in several
volumes.

Friends are
bookends
holding up
either side.

You
are my
friend.

You are
the time
worn
pages
of my
favorite
book.

you are my
watercolor
friend...

...you shine so bright –
even on a cloudy day.

You have a special way
of making everything easier
...my friend.

Aren't you amazing?

You are **every** color in a rainbow
(and that's a lot).

Aren't you simply the best there is?

You are the best kind of laughter
and the most gentle tears.

You are the task made clear
and the road paved before me.

You are my friend.

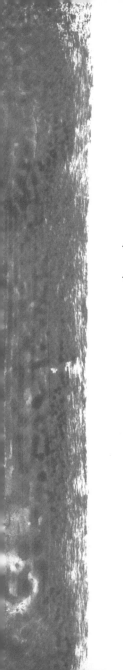

You are quite quirky,
we're bound to be good friends.

Just give me color.
Just let me dream.
Just have me stand by my friends
in peace:
then I shall know
what it is to be content.

Apparently
the angels were quite busy
so God sent you,
my friend, along.

Like bridges between mountains
comes the introduction of a friend.

The three-fold braid
of friendship is
need,
common want,
and acceptance.

needs seen
and met,
wants shared
and celebrated,
and acceptance
extended
with an
unqualified
clasp.

A new friend
expands experience
much like
a new idea
opens the mind.

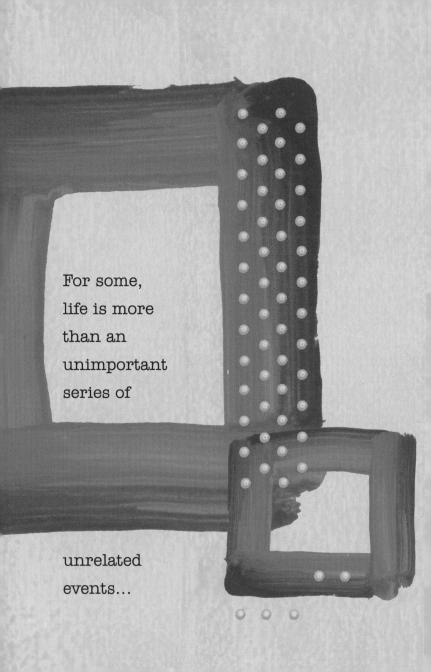

For some,
life is more
than an
unimportant
series of

unrelated
events...

...much more.

There are some people
who bring excellence
to each task
and sincerity
to each encounter...

...It's as though
they see a bigger
picture
to their days
which enables them
to overlook obstacles
and see opportunity.

Some people like you.

Smiles are
wordless
paragraphs
of friendship.

Friends see

what
is invisible:

hear
what
is not
spoken;

hold
space
for
intangibles.

Friendship is
both fragile
and durable,
at the same time.

Friends find ways
to deliver the harshest truth
in the most gentle way.

The kindness

of time
softens
the edges
of the most

pointed
of friendships.

my dear friend,
you are in my heart...

Always you may come to me
with whatever you hold –

laughter,
tears,
mischief,
anger,
affection,
seriousness,
silliness,
energy,
sorrow...

run it all by
and I'll try
to run with you.

I'll do my best
to be a castle for you:

A safe place.

I'll
always
do my best
to be
your
friend.

- Create plans and procedures.
- Establish timelines.
- Target completion.
- Purpose toward certain ends.

All good.

Friendship trumps them all
in a second...

and manages to get them done
faster, better, stronger.

A friend
is a brand new
Ferris Wheel
in the
amusement park:

new circles
and higher
perspectives.

When I have not
remembered
all that is good—

you have always **mirrored** my own goodness.

When I was unable to see –
you stood in front of me
and reflected my limitless possibility.

Thank you, my friend.

My pantry was empty
but my table
was full
of laughter
and the abundance
that only friendship nurtures.

If you ever need
to come in
from the rain

I'll be there
as your
warm home.

Feeding a friend
fills your own belly.

A flower
from the hand of a friend
never dies.

Over

the miles

of years

a voice calls

and I am

happy

to answer,

"Yes, sweet friend,

I remember you."

By confronting
the greatness of others
I am able to see
what I am capable of being.

In standing
before your integrity
I am called
to more careful
depths of being.

As I call upon you
I am grateful
there is a vastness
in our friendship.

Cultivate
the wild
and
growing garden
of
friendship...

...so that both
the garden
and the friend
are stronger
at the dusk
of the day
than at the
dawn.

My wizard friend:

you always

have a surprise

or two

to pull

out of your hat.

I see the fireworks
and colors
all the way
from your house
to mine.

You know
if you ever
need a place
to celebrate

I'll be there
to play
music
and dance.

I will sing the song of friendship

with the music
of loyalty and commitment.

Wear friendship
on your head,
it will keep the rain off.

I write the story
of my days
with the pen
of friendship...

...it is a volume that
begins with you.

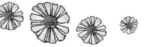

Dear Friend:

You are my good friend.

At your heart you are the best of everything. There is a gentleness which blows away all unkindness and leaves only the gem. All the qualities which first drew me to you spring from that heart-center. We must call each other to that place more often. Find creative ways to walk you to your best. Search for ways of reaching deep to find the qualities that promote personal growth and the greatest benefit to each other. When I look at you I see long standing loyalty, strength, quiet courage (much more than you think you have). Compassion. Patience (you always have an ear for me). You may lose sight of these qualities, but I see them, always.

I value the bond built between us. There are many tides to the river of our friendship: gladly I sail them all. It is with open arms I welcome you. It is sweet refreshment to have someone serve up the kind truth.

You demonstrate unconditional loving. I model your integrity, learn to challenge and overcome difficulties and become a stronger person. Friendship sustains me in times of uncertainty.

You speak eloquently and I remember my ideals. You speak support and I remember my own voice. You whisper possibility at the start of change and I remember one person makes a difference. Friendship is an inspired guide.

While instinct loses it's clarity in the press of immediate need, I want the best of all things for you. I celebrate you. Really! You are a party simply waiting to happen. A little bit party and sometimes a three ring circus but always a lot of fun. While I do not always understand you — I value you. Not simply acting on need — I want you. I do not care for you out of obligation or habit — I choose you. I accept you.

I have known the many names of friendship. It has been defined between us. It grows in spite of being named, "Distance." It is known as, "Festivity," for there is always a reason to rejoice. It is seen as, "Silence," for my friend has always stood with me in dark times, sacrificing comfort in order to comfort me. It is called, "Listening." My friend has known the words of my heart when I had not the ability to hear them myself.

By so many means, I know of friendship in knowing you.

Your Good Friend

When you have one friend,

you hold the hand
of the world.

Us. Friends: always.
Laughter.
A little chocolate.
A lot
of miles.

Secrets shared.
A few kind lies.
Stories.
Change.

Us: friends.
Always.

my friend, I wish for you the color that you bring forth in others to rise greatly within you. I wish you your own best strength. I wish you always to have good friends at your side. I wish you desired possibilities before you and contentment behind you. I wish you the beginnings of all your dreams and many of the ends. I wish you peace. I wish for you that fully collected moment when you become intimate with your own sufficiency, your wonder, your palmed possibility. From that exchange may you walk away content, satisfied with the sound of your own answers. May you wrap the gifts of your life with the ribbons of friendship and be amazed at every time that you return to hold your gifts.

acknowledgments

Barbara Ann and Jan Marie. Kathleen and Kim: you are the bookends holding the volumes of my life.

Jan, you lift my perspective. Liz you make my work sparkle. And you, the many friends, my collective "us," who will recognize their place in this work: thank you for helping me learn the many names of friendship and inspire others to honor the US in their lives and celebrate the power of friendship.

my dear friend,